AN AWFULLY BEASTLY BUSINESS

HUNTING FOR TROLLS

(An adaptation taken from
Bang Goes a Troll)

Written by The Beastly Boys
Adapted by Maureen Haselhurst
Illustrated by Jonny Duddle

Published by Pearson Education Limited, Edinburgh Gate, Harlow, Essex, CM20 2JE
Registered company number: 872828

www.pearsonschools.co.uk

Adapted text based on *Bang Goes a Troll*, originally published by Simon & Schuster
Children's Books in 2009.
Copyright © Matthew Morgan, David Sinden and Guy Macdonald 2009
Interior illustrations copyright © Jonny Duddle 2009
Cover illustration copyright © Jonny Duddle 2010

Adaptation by Maureen Haselhurst

Cover/interior illustrations and text all used by kind permission of Simon & Schuster
Children's Books.

The rights of Matthew Morgan, David Sinden and Guy Macdonald to be identified
as authors of this work have been asserted by them in accordance with the Copyright,
Designs and Patents Act 1988.

First published 2011

2020
10 9 8

British Library Cataloguing in Publication Data
A catalogue record for this book is available from the British Library

ISBN 978 1 408 27392 0

Printed and bound at Ashford Colour Press

Acknowledgements
We would like to thank the children and teachers of Bangor Central Integrated
Primary School, NI; Bishop Henderson C of E Primary School, Somerset;
Brookside Community Primary School, Somerset; Cheddington Combined School,
Buckinghamshire; Cofton Primary School, Birmingham; Dair House Independent
School, Buckinghamshire; Deal Parochial School, Kent; Newbold Riverside Primary
School, Rugby and Windmill Primary School, Oxford for their invaluable help in the
development and trialling of the Bug Club resources.

Every effort has been made to contact copyright holders of material reproduced in this
book. Any omissions will be rectified in subsequent printings if notice is given to the
publishers.

Visit the Beastly Business website for lots of exciting extras – meet the authors,
join the RSPCB and discover the secrets of the beasts...!

CONTENTS

Scamblesby C E Primary
School
Scamblesby
Louth
Lincs
LN11 9XG

Tel No: 01507 343629

ROYAL SOCIETY FOR THE PREVENTION OF CRUELTY TO BEASTS

·RSPCB·

"I DO SOLEMNLY
SWEAR TO PRESERVE
AND PROTECT THE
WILD. FROM THIS DAY
FORTH I PLEDGE MY
ALLEGIANCE
TO BEASTS."

CHAPTER ONE

High in the snowy northlands of Norway a mountain was exploding. Great tongues of flame whooshed and roared through the underground caves and thick, black smoke billowed out on the wind.

From inside the mountain came the sounds of underground beasts; growls and squeals; bellows and squawks.

Beasts were stampeding out from every tunnel, cave and crevice in the mountainside. Ice bears, vampire owls and giant spiders rampaged across the snow fields. Then came the tusked trolls – huge, green and dangerous; even they were terrified by the roaring inferno.

It might have been a volcano except for the notice nailed to a burnt pine tree.

BOOM 'N' BUST

MINING

CORPORATION

★　★　★

At the RSPCB, The Royal Society
for the Prevention of Cruelty to Beasts,
Ulf parked his quad bike outside an old
country mansion. This was Farraway
Hall, the headquarters of the RSPCB.

Although he looked like an ordinary
human boy, Ulf was beast blood. He
was a werewolf and, on the nights of
the full moon, he would change from
boy to wolf. Farraway Hall was his
home.

Dr Fielding, the RSPCB's vet, came
out of the house looking worried.

"Take a look at this, Ulf," she said,
handing him a newspaper.

BEASTLY NEWS

From our reporter Sally Mander

Something dastardly is afoot in a remote part of Norway. Honeycomb Mountain, home to the near-extinct Longtusk Trolls, is under threat.

The illegal mining operations of the Boom 'n' Bust Mining Corporation are blasting the mountain to smithereens.

The zillionaire President of B 'n' B, Mr Spender Rockybuster, said, "Hey – who cares about a few ugly-buglies? So, a few trolls go bang – what's so bad about that?"

"Can we rescue them, Dr Fielding?"
Ulf asked.

"We've got to, Ulf," Dr Fielding
replied. "I've already downloaded
the information from the computer.
They're mining Gemgold. It's
incredibly valuable and they'll stop at
nothing to get the stuff out. We've got
to save those beasts somehow."

"Is there room for them all at
Farraway Hall?" asked Ulf.

"We'll make room," Dr Fielding
said firmly.

Ulf went into the house. He made
his way up the shadowy staircase
and opened the door to the Room of
Curiosities. Researching on the internet
was all very well, but not everything
could be found online.

Half hidden in a dusty corner, he

found a box labelled 'Useful Bits and Bobs for Beastly Expeditions'. Unfortunately he couldn't open it as a small fairy was sitting on the lid.

"Hi, Tiana," Ulf smiled at her. "I need to look in that box. Can you move over?"

The fairy folded her arms. "Shan't!" she said defiantly.

"Why not?"

"I want to go on the troll rescue. I'll only move if you take me with you."

"It's far too dangerous, Tiana."

"A bit of danger sounds great to me," she retorted.

"Dr Fielding would never agree to it," Ulf told her. "Now, please can I open the box?"

"All right, but I'm coming anyway!" she sulked, and flew off in a huff.

A few minutes later, Ulf left the Room of Curiosities clutching an old canvas bag, a shiny silver compass and an old-fashioned metal head torch. Best of all he had found a tattered map of Honeycomb Mountain. It showed a web of underground tunnels and caverns, all with very sinister names.

★   ★   ★

Ulf found Dr Fielding standing next to the RSPCB helicopter. She was talking to a hulky giant.

"Hi, Orson," called Ulf.

Orson beamed at him. "I'm looking forward to this expedition. Longtusk Trolls are smashing little fellows."

Dr Fielding climbed into the cockpit and checked the flight controls. She looked down at Ulf and frowned.

"Are you sure you want to come with us, Ulf? It might be dangerous."

"Sure as sure." And he climbed into the passenger seat.

"Ready, Orson," she called back to the giant.

Orson was too big to fit inside the helicopter, so he flew under it, suspended on a foot strap at the end of a long, steel flying cable.

"Ready!" he yelled.

The engine roared into life, the blades began to turn and the helicopter lifted off.

Ulf felt the surge of speed as it turned north towards Honeycomb Mountain and adventure.

ROYAL SOCIETY FOR THE PREVENTION OF CRUELTY TO BEASTS · RSPCB ·

CHAPTER TWO

Ulf's ears popped as the helicopter descended. There was a clanking sound followed by a thud as Orson unclipped his flying cable and dropped onto the hard-packed snow. A few seconds later, the helicopter touched down.

Ulf and Dr Fielding jumped out and went round to find Orson. He was carrying a large gas lantern in his shovel-like hands.

Dr Fielding began to rummage through her backpack.

"I'll just check I've got everything I need," she said. "Yes, mobile phone, stethoscope, syringes, adrenaline and cotton wool. Right, that's fine. Let's go."

Ulf picked up his bag and squinted around. It was blowing a blizzard. Between the swirling snowflakes, he could just make out the dim entrances of the caves that dotted the mountainside. Dr Fielding and Orson were already heading away from the helicopter towards the nearest of them.

"Hurry up, Ulf. It's too cold to hang around," a tiny voice protested. The voice was coming from inside his bag. Ulf pulled it open and there, perched on the silver compass, was a tiny, glittering stowaway.

"Tiana!" he gasped.

"I said I was coming," she said.

"Well, stay in my bag," Ulf told her. "This is no place for a fairy."

"Oh, you never know, I might come in useful," she said, and she smiled brightly.

Ulf turned to go, but was distracted by a noticeboard nailed to a smoke-blackened pine tree.

PRIVATE BOOM 'N' BUST MINING CORPORATION

SCARPER! NICK OFF! LEG IT! KEEP OUT – OR ELSE!

"Uh-oh," he murmured and turned to follow Dr Fielding and Orson. They were disappearing into a cave. There were rocks around its entrance that looked like broken dragon's teeth.

"Wait for me!" he called.

Ulf wasn't worried about feeling the cold. He was nearing his transformation. His blood was warming up and the hair on his hands and feet was starting to thicken. Tonight the moon would be full and he'd change from boy to wolf.

He headed for the cave entrance and crept inside. He was surrounded by the chittering sounds of underground beasts. Tiny eyes on stalks peered out from every crack in the walls.

Way ahead of him, he could see the flickering light of Orson's lantern. It

turned off down a side tunnel.

★   ★   ★

Ulf found himself in a large chamber. Hanging from the roof were hundreds of long trunk-like creatures that glistened with phosphorescent light.

Tiana flew out again and darted between them. "They're beautiful," she said.

"Mind out," Ulf replied. He had seen pictures of these beasts. "They're elephant leeches. They can drink more blood than a vampire."

The little fairy squealed, then darted back into the safety of Ulf's bag.

The elephant leeches reached out towards him, rippling and swaying like elephants' trunks. One of them

clamped its fleshy sucker on his
shoulder.

"No you don't," Ulf said, shuddering.
He peeled the leech's sucker from his
T-shirt, then wove his way cautiously
between them, wading knee-deep in
piles of skin and bone.

At last he reached a narrow exit
at the far end of the chamber and
squeezed out into the darkness beyond.

★   ★   ★

He found himself in a tall cavern.
The torchlight picked out a vast mesh
of intertwined white silk ropes that
hung from the ceiling in a gigantic
web. In it dangled the limp bodies of
dead owls and vampire bats.

"Ulf, I don't like the look of this
place," Tiana said, peeking out from

Ulf's bag.

Ulf looked at the map again and realised too late where he was – the Spider's Larder!

He turned to make a dash for it, but something was already moving above his head. He looked up to see an enormous spider with hairy legs a metre long descending one of the ropes. It was glowing white with deadly venom. It dropped to the ground, hissing, and its jaws opened, exposing six mouths, each with razor-sharp fangs.

Ulf took to his heels and sprinted through the chamber with the spider scurrying after him.

The torchlight lit upon a large opening in the side of the tunnel. He dived inside and switched off his light just in time to see the spider's glowing white shape go scuttling past.

"Phew," he breathed.

But wait. Tap-tap-tap-tap. The beast was coming back.

Ulf saw a hairy leg step through the opening.

Oh no! he thought.

A loud grunting, snuffling sound came from behind him. The spider hissed, pulled back and scurried away.

Ulf tensed. Whatever had scared the spider away was too close for comfort. He sniffed. The cave stank of old meat and beast dung. He turned his torch on. He was crouching in a vast underground chamber, bigger than a barn and twice as high. All around him, staring from the shadows, were huge green trolls.

CHAPTER THREE

Ulf jumped to his feet, but the exit was blocked by an enormous male troll. More of the beasts were gathering on all sides. "Stay in my bag, Tiana," he warned her.

He was surrounded by over twenty trolls, the biggest he'd ever seen, with hairy chins and long tusks that grew from their lower lips.

They edged nearer, drooling and slobbering, dragging their knuckles along the ground.

Some began growling. Others stood upright beating their chests. "Oof! Oof! Oof!"

A huge male lumbered towards him, swiping out with its huge, clawed hand, its tusks ready to strike.

Ulf's head torch shone on its furious face and the troll stopped dead in its tracks, holding its arm up to shield its eyes.

"So, you don't like the light," said Ulf. He swung his head torch from one troll to the next. But as each troll stepped back, another edged forward. "Oof! Oof! Oof!"

Saliva was dribbling down their chins. Ulf closed his eyes and waited to be eaten.

Just then, footsteps came thumping

down the tunnel and lantern light flooded the chamber. It was Orson the giant!

"Orson! Thank goodness!" Ulf yelled.

Orson turned up the gas on his lantern. "They're beauties, aren't they, Ulf? But they can be a bit grumpy," he said, swinging the lantern towards them. "That's it. Back you go," and the trolls retreated to the edges of the chamber.

There were more footsteps and Dr Fielding came into the chamber, shining a torch.

"Ulf!" She sounded relieved. "Thank goodness we've found you."

She stopped and stared at the trolls. "Longtusks!" she said. "How magnificent."

There was the faintest rustle inside Ulf's bag and Tiana's tiny face peered out. "I'm missing all the fun," she whispered. "Don't worry, nobody will see me," and she flew into the shadows.

Dr Fielding was staring intently at the floor of the cave. It was covered in a thick layer of black soot. "What on earth has happened here?" she asked.

★   ★   ★

She looked more closely at the trolls. Some of them had blackened skin. An adult female was scraping soot from her stomach. A wrinkled old troll with broken tusks was chewing a sooty bone. A male was grooming a female, trying to clean black soot from her back.

"That mining corporation's to blame

for all this," Dr Fielding said angrily. "They've been using high-powered explosives. These poor beasts could have been burned alive in their caves."

"Look at that one, Dr Fielding," said Ulf, pointing to a big male troll. It was lying on the ground and a female was bending over it, licking its skin.

"Be careful, Doctor," Orson warned her. He swung his lantern from side to side and the female troll slowly backed away. "That's it, girl. Give us a little space."

Dr Fielding knelt down beside the motionless troll and inspected it.

Ulf watched her. "Is it alive?" he asked.

"It's still warm," replied Dr Fielding. "Can you help me roll it over, Ulf?"

They gripped the troll's tusks and

heaved, rolling it onto its back.

Dr Fielding pressed her ear to the troll's mouth and listened. "It's only just breathing," she said. She lifted its wrinkled eyelids to show its dull, clouded pupils. "It's barely conscious."

The troll coughed and sticky black mucus splattered its hairy chin. Dr Fielding prised its mouth open and shone her torch inside.

"Urgh," gasped Ulf. "Its breath stinks."

The troll's teeth were crooked and chipped, with bits of meat and fur stuck between them. Its tongue was thick and pitted. Its whole mouth was black with soot.

"It's been inhaling a lot of smoke," Dr Fielding said. "See how swollen its throat is."

Ulf looked to the back of the troll's mouth. The opening to its windpipe was constricted and its breathing sounded strained.

The troll snorted and more black mucus leaked from its nose.

"See if you can clear its nose, Ulf," said Dr Fielding, handing him a pack of cotton wool.

Ulf gagged and swallowed hard. Taking a wad of cotton wool, he put his finger up the troll's hairy nostrils and scooped out lumps of black gunk.

Dr Fielding held her stethoscope to the troll's chest and listened. "Its lungs sound blocked," she said.

The troll wheezed and choked, gasping for breath. It shuddered and then lay still.

"What's happening?" asked Ulf.

"It's stopped breathing!" Dr Fielding said.

The troll lay motionless, as if it were dead.

Dr Fielding felt its wrist, checking for a pulse. "Its heart's stopped. Stand back, Ulf."

Dr Fielding placed both hands on the centre of the troll's broad green chest. She interlocked her fingers and, with her arms straight, started pressing down hard, again and again.

"What are you doing?" Ulf asked.

"I'm trying to get his heart going again," Dr Fielding explained.

She put her hand under the troll's hairy chin and tilted its head back to open its windpipe. Then she covered its nose with both hands and took a deep breath.

Ulf watched as Dr Fielding opened her mouth over the troll's rubbery lips and steadily breathed into its mouth.

"Eyugh! She's kissing the troll!" Orson muttered.

"She's not. She's trying to help it breathe," Ulf explained.

★   ★   ★

Dr Fielding sat up and pushed
the troll's chest again. It still wasn't
moving. She took another breath and
placed her mouth over the troll's,
breathing into it.

"Come on, troll. You can do it," Ulf
said.

Dr Fielding blew once more into the
troll's mouth. Suddenly, it coughed and
its body convulsed. Dr Fielding pulled
her head away, wiping her lips.

The troll coughed, splattering out
more thick black mucus. It shook its
head. It was breathing!

Dr Fielding took a bottle and a
syringe from her rucksack and gave it
an injection of adrenaline.

The troll snorted and rolled over
onto all fours.

The rest of the trolls lumbered over

and patted him.

"Oof, oof!" they grunted, nodding their great heads. Somehow their Oofs sounded less threatening. The female shuffled towards Dr Fielding and stroked her arm. Then, one by one, the rest of the trolls did the same.

"I think you've made some new friends," chuckled Orson.

There was the faintest whirr of wings. "Trolls are really quite sweet," Tiana giggled and she darted back into Ulf's bag. No one noticed her, for it was then that an almighty explosion ripped through the mountain.

CHAPTER FOUR

Outside, on the snowy mountainside,
Spender Rockybuster from the
Boom 'n' Bust Mining Corporation
was hard at work. He was using
illegal ultra-high explosives to blast
Honeycomb Mountain apart.

"There are rich reserves of precious
Gemgold down there, and I want every
gram!" he cried.

The mountain trembled with each
new explosion, sending wild beasts

scurrying in terror from their lairs and hurtling off into the frozen wilderness.

"Get a look at those weirdos," jeered Spender Rockybuster. "So we're evicting them from their stinking dens – who cares!" He grasped the handle of his blasting box, yelling, "Five, four, three, two, one – Fire!" and the mountain trembled as another huge explosion ripped through its heart.

★　　★　　★

Inside the mountain, the trolls were panicking. They huddled together in one corner of the chamber, beating their chests.

Great cracks were opening up in the ceiling and chunks of fallen rock littered the floor. Orson put his huge arms above his head, supporting the roof with his hands, but it was too much even for a giant. "I can't keep this up much longer," he panted.

"We've got to get the trolls out of here or we'll all be crushed to death," Ulf shouted.

Ulf grabbed Orson's lantern and waved it at the trolls, herding them towards the entrance.

"Move it!" he shouted. "This place is going to collapse any moment now!"

The trolls seemed to understand and shuffled forwards.

Suddenly, there was a roaring sound and a ball of fire came scorching down the tunnel.

"Take cover!" Orson yelled. He ran to the entrance of the tunnel and threw his arms around Dr Fielding and Ulf, shielding them as the fireball screamed past. As he did, the cave ceiling began falling down. Great chunks of rock came crashing down into the trolls' home.

Ulf turned to go up the tunnel, but more flames were blazing along the tunnel walls. "We daren't go out that way now," he said. "There must be another exit."

He studied the old map and exclaimed, "Yes. There is another way out. Look!"

"Abandoned wagonway," Dr Fielding read.

Ulf scooted across the chamber to the back wall and there, in the light of his head torch, he saw it. Two parallel iron rails snaked out of the chamber. It was a railway track and on it stood a row of wooden wagons.

A whooshing sound erupted outside the Trolls' Chamber as another fireball torpedoed past. Thick black smoke was snaking in through the fallen rocks. The chamber was slowly but surely filling with smoke.

"Orson, get the trolls into the wagons," shouted Dr Fielding.

"Will do!" he bellowed.

The trolls didn't need any coaxing to get out of their chamber. They lumbered along the track and squeezed their hefty bodies into the rickety old wagons.

"Bunk over and let the lady have a seat," Orson said.

The big male troll squeezed along his seat and Dr Fielding slipped in next to him.

"I'll ride in the back!" shouted Orson, jumping onto the last wagon like a secret service minder.

"Who's going to drive this thing?" Ulf asked.

"You, of course," yelled Orson.

Ulf scrambled into the front wagon. He hadn't the foggiest idea how to make it move.

★ ★ ★

There were two pedals on the splintered wooden floor – the kind of thing he'd seen on kids' pedal cars. He pushed one pedal with one foot and then the second pedal with his other foot. And that was it – they were moving.

They juddered along slowly at first,

and then the railway track began to slope downhill and off they shot, faster and faster until the black tunnel walls were a blur.

"Yee-hah!" yelled Ulf. What an escape!

Through Honeycomb Mountain they rocketed, with the Longtusk Trolls turning greener than ever.

"Are we nearly there?" shouted Orson.

"Not far now," Ulf shouted back. "There's light ahead."

The rail track took a sharp curve uphill and they burst out into the outside world. It was a shining world, the ground silvered with snow and the sky spangled with stars.

"We've done it," beamed Dr Fielding. "Now let's get these wonderful beasts back to Farraway Hall and safety."

Ulf stared at her. "But how?"

Dr Fielding smiled and pointed up. Above them, the night sky was filled with the hum and whir of a score of helicopters. They flew like a swarm of wasp beasts over the summit of Honeycomb Mountain and dropped down, down, down onto the snowfields.

Orson leaped off his wagon and strode to the front of the train.

"It worked, Orson," said Dr Fielding.

"What worked?" asked Ulf.

"My mobile phone," she explained. "I managed to get a signal underground and ordered a fleet of helicopters from NICE."

NICE was the department for National and International Criminal

Emergencies. They were always called in when crimes against beasts were committed.

BOOOOOM!

A terrific explosion ripped through the mountain. The trolls in the wagons clutched one another in horror.

"Get them over to the helicopters, Orson!" shouted Dr Fielding. "The whole mountain's going to collapse."

Orson ran along the length of the wagons, waving his lantern at the trolls. They prised themselves out of the wagons, but instead of moving out of the tunnel, they turned around and headed back into the mountain.

"Stop them!" shouted Dr Fielding,

but it was no good. They stampeded
back into the darkness, terrified of the
light of the full moon that was starting
to rise over the glaring white snow.

CHAPTER FIVE

Dr Fielding glanced over at the helicopters. The pilots would only keep them there if it was safe to do so. If the huge explosions continued, they would take off, with or without her precious beasts.

Another bevy of blasts rattled the rocks around them.

"Do something, Ulf," she pleaded, knowing it was silly to expect a boy to perform a super-human feat.

Ulf was standing quietly by the wagonway. The huge full moon was shining down on him and he was staring at it in awe.

Ulf's eyes flashed silver. He felt the bones in his chest cracking. His skeleton was realigning. Dark hair sprouted over his whole body. A thick tail grew from the base of his spine. His nails lengthened into claws. His muscles bulged and fangs split through his gums.

Ulf looked the moon full in the face and howled.

"Go, werewolf! Go!" shouted Orson.

Ulf the werewolf turned his back on the helicopters and bounded back into the tunnel.

He caught up with the trolls some way back down the wagonway. They were in such a panic that they didn't notice him slinking past them.

The full moon lit the tunnel, as bright as a spotlight, as Ulf reared up in front of them.

Ulf snarled, showing a set of yellow teeth that could rip a troll hide into shreds. He reared up onto his hind legs, showing a set of claws that could gouge out a troll's eyes. One by one, he fixed them with his silver glare and one by one, each troll knew it had met its match.

A minute later, the herd of trolls trotted clumsily out of the tunnel towards the waiting helicopters, with Ulf at their heels.

Dr Fielding picked up Ulf's bag from

the mouth of the tunnel, where he had dropped it as he had transformed.

It was then that she saw a scowling man on skis skimming away across the snow.

Dr Fielding recognised him. She had seen his picture in the *Beastly News*.

"Stop, Mr Rockybuster! Quick, he's getting away!" she cried.

The men from NICE spotted him.

"Hold it, Rockybuster!" they shouted. "You're under arrest for cruelty to beasts."

Spender Rockybuster pushed off, his skis swishing over the snow. He was getting away.

Something shuffled inside Ulf's bag and out flew a tiny, winged creature.

"Tiana!" gasped Dr Fielding in amazement.

The fairy took to the air and darted off in pursuit.

As Rockybuster swooped down the mountainside, something glittering flew into his face. He swatted it away but it came back at him, its tiny wings buzzing in his eyes. He made a grab for it. His ski poles slipped from his grasp and slithered away. Now, he was out of control, pelting downhill and heading straight for a burnt pine tree.

CRASH!

Mr Spender Rockybuster had just collided with the BOOM 'N' BUST noticeboard.

"Gotcha!" the men from NICE cheered as they bundled him away.

★   ★   ★

The next morning, Ulf woke up in the RSPCB helicopter, wrapped in a blanket. He had transformed back into a boy.

Dr Fielding was flying the helicopter. Beside her was Tiana.

"Hey, you two," Ulf said, sitting up.

"Morning, Ulf," Tiana replied, flying to him. "We did it! We saved the trolls!"

Ulf looked out of the window and saw they were flying over the sea. In the distance he could see Farraway Hall and the beast park. He looked down and saw that Orson was hanging beneath the RSPCB helicopter on a flying rope. He waved and the giant gave him a thumbs up.

Behind them flew the NICE helicopters, the trolls tied carefully beneath them.

"Do you think they'll be at Farraway Hall for long?" Ulf asked.

"We'll look after them until they've recovered from the smoke," Dr Fielding said. "With Spender Rockybuster behind bars, it should be safe for them to return to their mountain very soon. Work has already begun on excavating new caves for them."

Ulf turned to Tiana. "By the way, Tiana," he said, "you were just great last night."

The fairy fluttered her wings. "Well, I did say that I might come in useful!"

THE END ... FOR NOW!